For you, Dad. Always. —MB

To all the wild animals, even if you only act like it. —DW

ACKNOWLEDGMENTS: Huge thanks to my editors: Karen Li, for your guidance and help in finding the "sass," and Sarah Howden, for your editing expertise and great sense of fun. And thank you to everyone at Owlkids, especially Karen B., Judy, Katherine, and Allison. I'm grateful to the incredibly talented Dave Whamond, whose wonderful illustrations bring this book to life, and to Alisa Baldwin for an awesome design. And thank you to Janice Weaver for your helpful edits. My thanks to the Ontario Arts Council for your generous support of this project through the Writers' Reserve. Thanks Mom, for so many reasons. And, as always, thank you to Sam and Grace for being perfectly wild.

Text © 2019 Maria Birmingham | Illustrations © 2019 Dave Whamond

Owlkids Books acknowledges the financial support of the Canada Council for the Arts, the Ontario Arts Council, the Government of Canada through the Canada Book Fund (CBF) and the Government of Ontario through the Ontario Creates Book Initiative for our publishing activities.

Published in Canada by Owlkids Books Inc., 1 Eglinton Avenue East, Toronto, ON M4P 3A1
Published in the US by Owlkids Books Inc., 1700 Fourth Street, Berkeley, CA 94710

Library of Congress Control Number: 2018963671

Library and Archives Canada Cataloguing in Publication

Birmingham, Maria, author
Acting wild : how we behave like birds, bugs, and beasts / by Maria Birmingham
; illustrated by Dave Whamond.

Includes bibliographical references.
ISBN 978-1-77147-326-2 (hardcover)

1. Human beings--Animal nature--Juvenile literature. 2. Human-animal relationships--Juvenile literature. 3. Animal behavior--Juvenile literature.
I. Whamond, Dave, illustrator II. Title.

GN280.7.B57 2019   j599.9   C2018-906451-X

Edited by Sarah Howden | Designed by Alisa Baldwin

Manufactured in Shenzhen, Guangdong, China, in March 2019, by C & C Offset
Job #HT1209

A   B   C   D   E   F

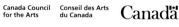

 Publisher of Chirp, Chickadee and OWL
www.owlkidsbooks.com | Owlkids Books is a division of bayard canada

ACTING WILD

How We Behave Like Birds, Bugs, and Beasts

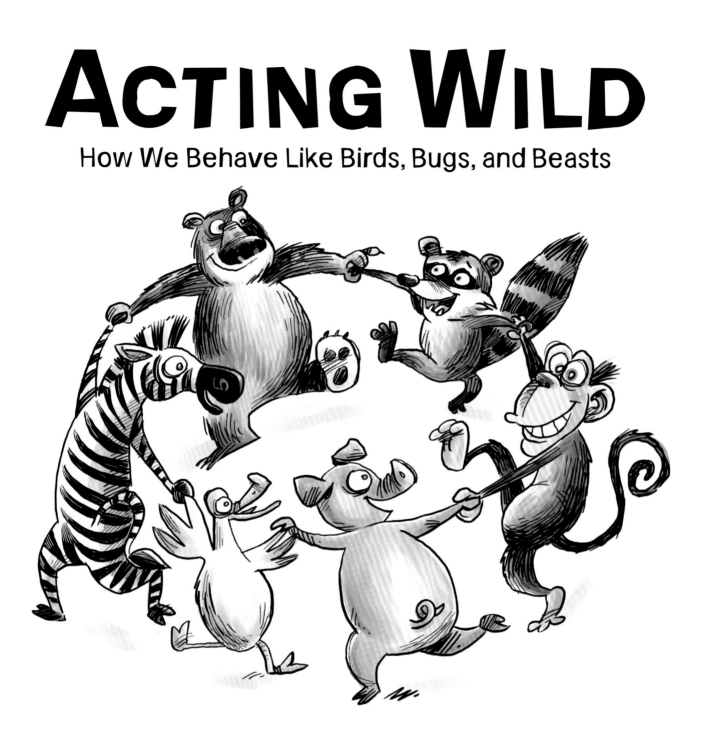

By **Maria Birmingham**

Illustrated by **Dave Whamond**

Owlkids Books

Contents

It's true. You're a member of a species called *Homo sapiens*, which means you're a primate—just like a chimpanzee, a baboon, and a lemur.

So you, dear human, are officially part of the animal kingdom. And that makes us relatives. Really, really, *REALLY* distant relatives. But relatives nonetheless. And like relatives, we animals have plenty of things in common.

Don't believe me?

C'mon, let's journey through the wild to see how you behave just like an animal. I guarantee that you'll soon see the family resemblance.

Let It Grow

Glad you decided to come along!

So where to begin?

How about food?

Back in the day, your ancestors moved around, always looking for their next meal. But once they discovered they could grow their own crops and raise their own livestock, they said goodbye to wandering and settled in one spot. And that was the beginning of farming.

But farming isn't only for humans. Many animals, including my very own cousins, are top-notch farmers, too.

APHID EGGS

Round 'Em Up

It's easy to see how farmer ants got their name. These ants raise aphids—little green bugs that eat sap from plants and leave behind a sugary liquid called honeydew. Farmer ants love to drink this sweet stuff. Sometimes they even "milk" the aphids for a honeydew meal!

Farmer ants carefully look after their herd. They protect the aphids' eggs as if they were their own, keep predators away, and carry the bugs to leafy pastures where they'll have plenty to eat.

Hair's to Farming

The hairy bristles that cover the yeti crab's claws make it look like a relative of the Abominable Snowman. But rather than being a monster from the deep, the shaggy-armed crab is a farming pro. Found off the coast of Costa Rica, it grows bacteria in the hair on its claws. This is the crab's main food source. To help the bacteria sprout, the deep-sea crab slowly waves its claws through the water. This allows nutrients to wash over the bacteria and speeds their growth.

Keep Off My Crops!

You could say damselfish are the gardeners of the sea. These small fish can digest only a specific red algae species called *Polysiphonia*. To make sure they have enough of these special algae, damselfish spend their days removing other unwanted algae species from coral reefs. The fish use their mouths to pluck these "weeds," tossing them far from their gardens. By weeding, damselfish give their favorite algae plenty of room to grow. They are so protective of their crop, they'll chase off fish that swim too close. They'll even attack human divers who swim near their gardens!

Other animals that farm: termites, spotted jellyfish, and salt marsh snails

That'll Teach You

You may have caught a glimpse of my ant pals and me at your school, crowding around a crumb in the corner of your classroom while your teacher is giving lessons.

Of course, that doesn't mean teaching isn't important to creatures in the animal kingdom. Sure, there aren't any desks or Smart Boards out in the wilderness, but there are still lessons to learn and teachers to teach them.

ANTEGERS

This Is How We Do It

In the deserts of southern Africa, adult meerkats teach their pups the ins and outs of capturing their favorite meal: scorpions. Since these critters can deliver a life-threatening sting, adults must show their young how to hunt them safely. At first, the older meerkat captures a scorpion, kills it, and gives it to the pup. Next step: the adult offers the young meerkat a scorpion with its stinger removed for the pup to kill by itself. When the pupil is about three months old, it's presented with its final lesson: a scorpion with its stinger intact. By this point, the pup has learned how to safely take down this meal on its own. That deserves an A+!

What's the Password?

Fairy wrens begin teaching their babies before they even hatch. A mother fairy wren sings her eggs a special song containing one unique chirp that becomes the family "password." When the nestlings hatch, they must chirp the note they learned from Mom to be fed. Why the need for a password? It's how Mom recognizes her babies. Some cuckoo species lay their eggs in fairy wrens' nests to get out of caring for their young. To make sure she's feeding her own hatchlings first, Mama Wren listens for her chicks to sing the family password. Then dinner is served!

Follow Me!

If you saw my second cousins—or as you humans call them, rock ants—scampering across the ground, you probably wouldn't realize that there's teaching going on. But these ants pair up in a buddy system—one is a teacher and the other a student that follows behind. The teacher shows the student a route from their nest to a new food source. During the lesson, the teacher ant runs slower than usual, allowing the student to keep up and learn the route. Once the ant knows the path to the food, it'll teach another bug from its colony in the same way.

Other animals that teach: chimpanzees, bottlenose dolphins, cheetahs, and golden lion tamarins

Laugh It Up

Just like you, animals enjoy a good chuckle. Here's one of *my* favorite jokes: Why was the baby ant confused? Because all her uncles were ants! Get it?

When it comes to you humans, researchers say laughter is a natural instinct. Babies begin to laugh shortly after birth. And while a good joke can get you ha-ha-ha-ing, studies show that you laugh mostly during conversations that aren't all that funny. It's a way for you to bond with others. Who knew?

CHIRP

LAB

It's Doggone Funny

Dog lovers don't need anyone to tell them that man's best friend yuks it up. But animal researcher Patricia Simonet set out to prove just that. She placed a microphone in parks where dogs were at play so she could capture their sounds. When she studied the recordings, Simonet found that the dogs made a unique laughing sound—similar to panting—as they played. While humans may not recognize a dog's laughter, other canines sure do. Simonet played the recorded laughs for puppies, and the sound made them excited and playful.

Rats ... I Can't Stop Laughing

Imagine a rat's laugh. You might think it'd sound like a sinister snarl. But an Estonian scientist found that young rats let out a sweet chirping while they're playing. During their research, Jaak Panksepp and his team tickled young rats on the nape of the neck. (They chose the neck because that's the place rats focus on while they're playing together.) The rats let out sounds that the scientists determined were laughter. Of course, rat laughs sound nothing like human laughs. In fact, they don't sound like anything at all! The human ear can't pick up the sound, so a special machine was needed to hear the chirp-like chuckling.

That's No Laugh

There are two animals that often sound like they're laughing, but it turns out their giggles are deceiving. The spotted hyena—sometimes called the laughing hyena—makes a noise that sounds like a human cackle. Research has shown, however, that this "laugh" is simply a noise they produce when they're excited, frustrated, or afraid. And the laughing kookaburra, an Australian bird, gets its name from its loud laughter-like call. But its song is just that—a song.

Other animals that laugh: chimpanzees, orangutans, and bonobo monkeys

13

Dealing with Death

Mind if we get serious for a moment? You know that life isn't all rainbows and unicorns, right? Humans go through sad times. They face difficult situations and lose people they love. That's when they feel a deep sadness known as mourning.

It turns out mourning isn't just for fancy mammals like you. Many animals also show signs of grief when they lose a member of the family.

>SNIFF<

When the Herd Hurts

Elephants live in close-knit herds made up of related females and offspring. So it makes sense that these gentle beasts are deeply affected by a death in the family. Scientists have seen elephants gathering around the body of a dead family member and gently touching it with their trunks. Sometimes they guard the body for days, refusing to move. Perhaps most surprising is that they may cover their departed companion with branches, grass, and soil, as if to bury it.

I'LL NEVER FORGET BOB!

ELEPHANTS NEVER FORGET...

HONK

Birds of a Feather

When a scrub jay comes across a dead jay, it lets out a loud screeching call to summon other birds to the area. They fly in and gather on trees near the body. Then the entire group begins to sing loudly over the dead jay. According to experts at the University of California, these noisy "funerals" can last anywhere from a few seconds to as long as thirty minutes.

Pets That Mourn

An American scientist named Barbara J. King has found evidence that dogs feel grief. King says that in a house with two pooches, it's common for one to mourn after its companion dies. The dog left behind may search the house over and over for its pal, looking in places where they spent time together. And it may go days without eating, sleeping, or playing. There are also stories of dogs mourning their owners. For instance, an Akita named Hachikō greeted his owner after work every day at a train station in Japan. After Hachikō's owner died, the loyal pet returned to the station each day until his own death nine years later.

Other animals that mourn: wolves, chimpanzees, bison, Atlantic spotted dolphins, and giraffes

15

Creature Construction

I love my home. It's the only place where I can kick back and put up my legs—all six of them!

For human folk, a house is also a place to relax. But you need shelter for other reasons, too. From the earliest times, you've relied on it to protect you from weather, other animals, and enemies.

Well, guess what? You're not alone. There are some seriously talented builders in the wild world, and they know a thing or two about creating a home sweet home.

FOR SALE

Home Is Where the Mound Is

Termite mounds dot the landscapes of Africa, Australia, and South America. Built by colonies numbering in the thousands, these mounds often reach crazy heights—some as tall as a giraffe! Termites can spend up to five years building the structure with soil, saliva, and their own poop. But believe it or not, they don't live in the mound. Instead, they make their home in an underground nest below it. The mound does have a purpose, though. A large chimney in the center stretches from the nest to the top of the mound. It acts like our lungs, taking in fresh air and pushing out stale air to keep the colony from suffocating underground.

I've Got a Gnawing Feeling

Beavers change their environment more than any other creature around. And they do it by building up a storm. These sharp-toothed rodents fell trees alongside lakes and rivers to build dams and create ponds. A beaver family then works together to strengthen the dam using twigs, branches, stones, and mud. Soon the master builders get to work on their next project. (There's a reason we say "busy as a beaver"!) They use more branches and mud to construct an island home called a lodge. It provides shelter in harsh weather and keeps beavers safe from predators.

The Buzz on Building

Wasps not only build their own nests but also make their own building materials from scratch! A colony's queen creates paper by chewing up bits of wood fiber and plants. Then she uses her saliva to soften the paper and transform it into a spongy pulp. When she finds a spot for the nest, the queen spits out her mouthful of pulp. Construction has begun! She does this over and over. Once the nest is big enough, worker wasps shape the inside, creating cells to house some very important tenants—the colony's eggs and babies! As the pulp dries, it hardens into a strong waterproof home.

Other animals that build: trapdoor spiders, bowerbirds, fire ants, and cichlid fish

ACTUALLY, I HAVE A FEW MORE CHANGES.

Tools of the Trade

Don't mind me. I'm just building an end table. Yeah, that's right. I know my way around a toolbox.

Truth is, you humans are pretty smart, too. Think about all the tools your species has created—forks for eating, pens for writing, hammers for building ... And that's just scratching the surface.

Believe it or not, there are animals in the wild that are just as creative. They see a problem to solve and find a tool to help them out.

CARPENTER ANT

BUGS ON A STICK

Fishing for Dinner

Scientist Jane Goodall has spent years studying chimpanzees in the wild. In the 1960s, she observed a male chimp using a stick to nab his dinner. The creature bent the twig and removed its leaves, then stuck it into a termite mound and slowly pulled it out. The twig was covered in termites, which the chimp gobbled up. Goodall couldn't believe her eyes—this was an animal using a tool. But after more research, she saw other chimps do the same thing. Yum!

Nosing Around

A group of bottlenose dolphins off the coast of Australia uses a special tool to hunt. The mammals tear a cone-shaped sponge from the seafloor and put it over the end of their beaks, sort of like pulling a glove on a hand. Then the dolphins use their beaks to dig into the seafloor, stirring up the fish that live there. Once the fish begin swimming around, the dolphins drop the sponge and catch their dinner. According to researchers from the University of Zurich, the dolphins have figured out that the sponge protects their beaks from the rocks and broken coral on the seafloor.

RAT-A-TAT TAT TAT

KEEP IT DOWN, BUDDY!

KNOCK KNOCK

WHO'S THERE?

You Otter See This

What's a sea otter's tool of choice? A rock. It's simple, but it gets the job done! The otter likes to eat hard-shelled prey like clams, mussels, and snails. Cracking open these shells to get at the soft food inside is not easy. So the sea otter grabs a rock and hammers away to break them open. The otter often does this while floating on its back, resting the shell on its chest. It even has a loose pouch under each forearm where it can store a favorite rock until it's needed—like a built-in tool belt!

Other animals that use tools: octopuses, ants, elephants, crocodiles, crows, and gorillas

Join the Conversation

Just a sec. A ... n ... d ... done. Sorry about that. It's hard to type without thumbs!

Of course, you humans don't have that problem. And you sure know how to communicate—texting, talking, sign language, video chats, letters, emails. It's all very impressive.

However, word on the street is that other species have found their own ways to keep in touch, by using their voices and even their bodies.

HEY, FRANK. FIVE-FOOT-EIGHT HUMAN HEADING YOUR WAY, 3.2 MILES PER HOUR. STAY ALERT!

All the Right Moves

Honeybees perform what's known as a waggle dance to communicate. Their dance moves tell other bees the exact location of a food source. When a bee finds a plentiful food supply, it returns to the hive and performs its dance for its hive-mates. The bee walks in a straight line, shaking its abdomen from side to side. It then dances in a figure-eight pattern. These moves tell its colony pals the direction and distance of the food so they can find it, too.

The Call of the Wild

Prairie dogs use a variety of sounds to communicate with one another, including barks, chirps, squeaks, and squeals. According to biologist Con Slobodchikoff, who's been studying prairie dogs for over thirty years, each sound they make has its own meaning. In fact, Slobodchikoff believes prairie dogs have a vocabulary of about one hundred "words" that they use to pass along information to their colony. Some calls alert their pals to an approaching predator. And these calls are so specific that they include details about the predator's speed and direction of travel. Amazingly, all this information is packed into a call that lasts less than one second!

Knock on Wood

Normally, banging your head against a tree will give you nothing but a headache. For the woodpecker, however, this is its preferred method of communication. The bird quickly taps its beak against trees and even metal objects in a distinctive pattern. This drumming, as it's called, is used to attract a mate, defend its territory, or warn that a predator is near. And the woodpecker gets its point across quickly—with at least twenty-five taps per second!

Other animals that communicate: bonobo monkeys, elephants, parrots, titi monkeys, and cuttlefish

Cleanse Whistl

Oops, sorry—you just caught me towelling off! Grooming—or making yourself clean and neat—is common throughout the animal kingdom. Just think how often your parents ask you to brush your teeth, comb your hair, or take a bath. Cleanliness helps keep you free from disease—and stink-free, too.

While I finish up, why don't you read how a few of the world's animals find a way to spruce themselves up.

RUBBA DUB DUB

Dentists of the Deep

Sometimes you humans need an expert to groom those hard-to-reach places. And animals are no different. For example, several fish species rely on cleaner shrimp to help them out. These crustaceans clean parasites from inside the mouths of the fish. To do this, the shrimps set up "cleaning stations" around coral reefs, and fish stop by to have them pick their teeth clean. It's the tooth!

FLOSS MUCH?

Monkey See, Monkey Groom

Chances are your dentist has told you that flossing your teeth is important. And four out of five macaque monkeys agree! Scientists at the University of Kyoto have discovered at least two types of macaques that floss their teeth. Japanese macaques pull out a strand of their own hair and run it back and forth between their teeth to remove food particles. Sometimes they'll floss with twigs, feathers, or coconut fibers instead. But get this: some long-tailed macaques in Thailand floss with human hair! These monkeys live near a shrine and will pull out the hair of people visiting the temple—ouch!—and then use it as dental floss.

Letting the Clean Cat Out of the Bag

Cats are serious when it comes to keeping their coats clean. According to experts, felines spend about half their waking hours grooming themselves. They use their tongues to lick themselves clean, often wetting their front paws with saliva and using those to do the job, too. This need to stay clean is likely an instinct. Cats are descended from the African wildcat, and they still have some of the behaviors of their ancestors. That includes licking away scents to make sure they aren't detected by prey.

Other animals that groom: birds, African helmeted turtles, primates, cockroaches, zebras, and horses

It's All Fun and Games

There's nothing like rounding up your friends to play a favorite sport or game. My ant pals and I just can't get enough of the eleven-legged race!

Scientists say play is an ancient instinct that's found in all mammals, as well as a lot of other creatures. In the case of humans, it helps you create social bonds with others and learn new skills. Other animals may play for the exact same reasons.

WOO-HOO!

Roo with the Punches

When baby kangaroos, called joeys, leave Mom's pouch, they're ready for playtime. The joeys like to play-fight with other young roos—and even with their mother. The kangaroos wrestle and bat each other with their paws, and may kick, too. Of course, when they spar with Mom, she takes it easy on the young joeys. She throws gentle jabs at her roos because she knows it's all in good fun.

Hitting the Slopes

For ravens in northern Canada and Alaska, nothing beats a fresh snowfall. Biologists from the University of Vermont have observed the ravens regularly sliding down steep snow-covered roofs. After zipping down the snowy slope, they walk or fly back to the top, and then slip-slide their way to the bottom again and again. Wheee! And ravens in Maine have been spotted playing in the snow, too. They roll down small piles of the cold white stuff, behaving more like puppies than birds.

Eight Times the Fun

What's an octopus to do with all those arms? Play, of course. Scientists from a university in Japan wanted to see if octopuses ever goof around. So they studied a group of fourteen that had been captured in the wild. The researchers gave the sea creatures Lego pieces and observed their reaction. While many animals ignore strange objects once they realize they aren't food and don't pose a danger, the octopuses were curious. They began to push and pull the blocks through the water, and tossed them from arm to arm. After watching them for days, the scientists concluded that the octopuses were playing with the Lego pieces as if they were toys.

WHAT A SHOW-OFF!

Other animals that play: dogs, chimpanzees, crocodiles, horses, herring gulls, and cats

This Calls for Teamwork

Can I get a hand here? Even an ant with six legs needs help once in a while!

You humans know all about working together to get a task done. Cooperation is such an important skill that your teacher even comments about it on your report card.

When we work together, things go much more smoothly. I guess that's why creatures of all types—from birds to bats—find ways to cooperate in the wild.

The Call to Cooperate

When a predator gets too close to a pied flycatcher's nest, this small bird doesn't hide or fly off. Instead, it screeches loudly at its attacker. This cry alerts other flycatchers in the area. They swoop over and form a mob that chases away the predator. Now that's what you call cooperation! But any flycatcher that doesn't help out its feathered friends had better be prepared to defend its own nest in the future. Researchers say a flycatcher will help its neighbor only if that bird answered its call for help in the past.

This Barf's for You

Who would have thought that bats know sharing is caring? A biologist from the University of Maryland has learned that female vampire bats, which feed on the blood of birds and cattle, share their food with others. Each night, they set out on a hunt for dinner. But some will have no success, and a bat can starve if it goes without a meal for even two nights. Not to worry! Female vampire bats are happy to share their spoils with those who come home hungry. They throw up some of the blood they ate and let hungry bats lick a meal right off their faces. (Mmmm ... bat barf.) Yes, it's gross. But if the females didn't step up, the species wouldn't survive.

I'll Lead the Way

They may be two different species, but the moray eel and the grouper are all about cooperation. A scientist from a Swiss university found that the pair will cooperate to nab a meal. While snorkeling, the scientist watched as a grouper swam over and shook its head in a moray eel's face. Then the pair swam off together, with the grouper leading the eel to prey hiding among some rocks. The eel slipped between the rocks and grabbed the prey. The scientist watched other eels and groupers do the same thing. Sometimes the moray eel ate the prey, and other times it let its grouper pal gobble it up.

Other animals that cooperate: ants, cleaner fish, wolves, and meerkats

27

Time for a Trip

Whew! Once we finish this book, I'm going to need a vacation.

If I were a human, I could jet off on a plane. Or ride the rails. Or settle into a car for a road trip. But it's hard to make travel plans without a vehicle. You have no idea how easy you've got it.

I guess I shouldn't give you all the glory, though. Other animals have come up with their own ways to travel—from soaring to sailing to surfing.

STRONG WINDS FROM THE WEST...

We Have Liftoff

With all those legs, you'd think spiders wouldn't need to find any other way to get around. But it turns out some of them go ballooning! To take flight, a spider stands on its tiptoes and points its abdomen toward the sky. Then it releases a strand of silk, which catches the wind. And before you know it, it's up, up, and away! The spider takes to the sky, dangling beneath its silk thread. Ballooning spiders may travel short distances or hundreds of miles—it all depends on the wind. And these spiders are experts at air travel. Before they attempt a takeoff, they check the wind speed with the tiny hairs on their legs.

Let's Set Sail

When rising water threatens my pals the Alpine silver ants, these bugs build a raft. And not just any old raft—one made of ants! Scientists from a university in Switzerland discovered that the worker ants gather up the colony's eggs and babies and arrange them into the base of their vessel. Then they climb aboard, link their bodies together, and hold on to the younglings with their mouths to keep the raft from breaking apart. The queen ant is then placed in the center of the raft. While it may seem like a dangerous voyage for the young ants, they are perfectly fine when they reach their final destination.

Surf's Up!

Saltwater crocodiles aren't the best swimmers, especially over long distances. So what's a croc to do? Bodysurf, of course! Scientists studying crocodiles in the South Pacific found that the reptiles move from island to island by catching waves like surfers do. The crocs pay attention to the ocean currents, figuring out the best time to ride the waves and when to stop for a break. These bodysurfing trips can last over three weeks, with the crocodiles often traveling hundreds of miles. Experts aren't sure why they hit the surf for these long-distance journeys. But it's likely they're searching for prey or mates.

Other animals that travel: Adélie penguins, brine flies, and mother-of-pearl caterpillars

Animals of the World, UNITE!

So there you have it. You, kind reader, are an animal. And naturally, you behave like one.

You thought I was pretty out there, didn't you? C'mon, you thought I—a teeny, tiny speck of an ant—couldn't possibly know anything about you or the great big world.

But I think I proved my point. You humans are like so many creatures in the animal kingdom—whether it's a monkey in the jungle, an eel in the ocean, or a raven on a snowy rooftop.

Kind of takes your breath away, doesn't it?

So next time you see an ant scurrying across the ground or a squirrel in the park or any other member of the animal kingdom, maybe you can extend a greeting with a smile or a simple nod of the head. After all—from the smallest bug to the largest mammal—we're all part of one amazing family.

CAN YOU THINK OF ANY OTHER WAYS THAT PEOPLE BEHAVE **JUST LIKE ANIMALS?**

GLOSSARY

ANCESTOR — A person who lived generations ago and who you are related to

ANIMAL — Complex living thing that can move and respond to changes around it; includes bugs, wildlife, and humans

BACTERIA — Single-celled organisms that live on, in, or around us

BEAVER DAM — A structure made by beavers from logs and sticks to block the flow of a stream or river

BONDING — Creating a lasting connection between individuals

COLONY — A group of animals or insects living and working together

COMMUNICATION — Sharing information from one individual to another

HERD — A group of animals living together

HUMAN — An animal of the species *Homo sapiens* known for walking upright, complex thought, and forming societies

INSTINCT — A way of behaving, feeling, or thinking that is not learned

MOURNING — Showing sorrow after a loss

PARASITES — Plants or animals that live on or in other living things and feed off them

PREDATOR — An animal that hunts or kills other animals

PRIMATE — A type of mammal with a larger brain, the ability to grasp with hands or feet, and binocular vision

SPECIES — A scientific grouping for creatures with similar traits

SUGGESTED READING

Broom, Jenny. *Animalium: Welcome to the Museum.* Big Picture Press, 2014.

Buckley, Jr., James. *Animal Atlas.* Animal Planet, 2016.

Burnie, David. *The Animal Book: A Visual Encyclopedia of Life on Earth.* DK Publishing, 2013.

Castaldo, Nancy F. *Beastly Brains: Exploring How Animals Think, Talk, and Feel.* Houghton Mifflin Harcourt, 2017.

Cotton, Katie. *Counting Lions: Portraits from the Wild.* Candlewick, 2015.

Harvey, Derek. *Animal Antics.* DK Publishing, 2014.

Jenkins, Steve. *Animals by the Numbers: A Book of Infographics.* HMH Books for Young Readers, 2016.

Kelsey, Elin. *Wild Ideas: Let Nature Inspire Your Thinking.* Owlkids Books, 2015.

Stewart, Melissa. *Pipsqueaks, Slowpokes, and Stinkers: Celebrating Animal Underdogs.* Peachtree Publishers, 2018.

Wagner, Tricia Martineau. *50 Wacky Things Animals Do: Weird and Amazing Animal Facts.* Walter Foster, Jr. Publishing, 2017.

Woodward, John. *Animal! The Animal Kingdom as You've Never Seen It Before.* DK Publishing, 2016.